THE moon

CHRIS OXLADE

Heinemann
LIBRARY
Chicago, Illinois

www.capstonepub.com
Visit our website to find out
more information about
Heinemann-Raintree books.

To order:

☎ Phone 800-747-4992

🖳 Visit www.capstonepub.com
 to browse our catalog and order online.

Edited by Nancy Dickmann and Laura Knowles
Designed by Steve Mead
Illustration on p. 21 by Jeff Edwards
Original illustrations © Capstone Global
 Library Ltd 2013
Picture research by Mica Brancic

Originated by Capstone Global Library Ltd
Printed and bound in China by CTPS

16 15 14 13 12
10 9 8 7 6 5 4 3 2 1

**Library of Congress Cataloging-in-
 Publication Data**
Oxlade, Chris.
 The moon / Chris Oxlade.—1st ed.
 p. cm.—(Astronaut travel guides)
 Includes bibliographical references and index.
 ISBN 978-1-4109-4572-3 (hb)—ISBN 978-1-
4109-4581-5 (pb) 1. Moon—Juvenile literature.
I. Title.
 QB582.0954 2013
 523.3—dc23 2011039066

Acknowledgements
We would like to thank the following for
permission to reproduce photographs: Corbis
pp. 8 (© Bettmann), 7 (© Sunset Boulevard),
ESA p. 5 bottom and 18 (NASA); © ESA-CNES-
ARIANESPACE p. 27 (Optique Vidéo du CSG/JM
Guillon); John Spencer p. 34; NASA pp. 4 (JPL),
5 middle and 30 (Johnson Space Center), 5 top
and 17 (Headquarters), 11 (Ames Research
Center/Northrup Grumman), 16 (Johnson Space
Center), 20 (Johnson Space Center), 22 (Johnson
Space Center), 23 (Johnson Space Center), 25
(Johnson Space Center), 26 (Johnson Space
Center), 28, 29, 37, 38. Science Photo Library
pp. 9 (Omikron), 10 (Detlev Van Ravenswaay),
12 (NASA), 15 (Eckhard Slawik), 31 (NASA);
Shutterstock pp. 32 (© Ismael Jorda), 40-41
(© Martiin/Fluidworkshop).

Design image elements reproduced with
permission of Shutterstock/© Diego Barucco/
© Rafael Pacheco/© Reistlin Magere.

Cover photograph of the Earth and Moon
reproduced with permission of Shutterstock/
© Ibooo7.

We would like to thank John Spencer, Paolo
Nespoli, and the ESA for their invaluable help in
the preparation of this book.

Every effort has been made to contact copyright
holders of material reproduced in this book.
Any omissions will be rectified in subsequent
printings if notice is given to the publisher.

CONTENTS

Destination Moon 4

The Moon in History 6

Moon Science 12

Interview with an Astronaut 18

Astronauts on the Moon 20

Planning a Moon Mission 26

Interview with a
    Space Scientist 34

On the Moon 36

Map of the Solar System 40

Timeline 42

Fact File................................. 43

Glossary................................. 44

Find Out More 46

Index 48

Some words are shown in bold, **like this**. You can find out what they mean by looking in the glossary.

DON'T FORGET

These boxes will remind you what you need to take with you on your big adventure.

NUMBER CRUNCHING

Don't miss these little chunks of data as you speed through the travel guide!

AMAZING FACTS

You need to know these fascinating facts to get the most out of your space safari!

WHO'S WHO?

Find out about the space explorers who have studied the universe in the past and today.

DESTINATION MOON

How often have you looked up at the Moon in the night sky? Have you looked through a **telescope** to see its surface covered with **craters**? The Moon is our closest neighbor in space, and it is the only object in space that astronauts have visited. Have you wondered what it would be like to visit the Moon? This is the place to find out!

Looking at the Moon from Earth through a small telescope or large binoculars reveals a world littered with deep craters and dark patches called seas.

WHY VISIT THE MOON?

There are plenty of good reasons to visit the Moon. For a start, you can find out about Moon rocks and what is inside the Moon. This can help us to learn about how the Earth was formed. You can also look for places to build a Moon base, from which we could launch a mission to Mars in the future.

The Moon is simply an amazing place to visit. Things to see on the **lunar** surface include giant craters, enormous flat "seas" of frozen **lava**, mountains, and **canyons**. Just imagine walking across the dusty surface of the Moon and looking up to see Earth in the sky. Only 12 people have ever stood on the Moon. Could you be the next?

Turn to page 17 to find out what to expect when you take your first steps on the Moon.

Get tips on what to pack for your journey on pages 30–31.

Discover what life is like in space from astronaut Paolo Nespoli on page 18.

AMAZING FACTS

No country owns the Moon or any part of the Moon. So no need to take a passport! The Outer Space Treaty is an international agreement made in 1967 that says no country can claim the Moon as its own, and that the Moon can only be used for peaceful purposes.

THE MOON IN HISTORY

Humans must have looked up at the Moon for hundreds of thousands of years. But until telescopes were invented in the 1600s, people knew little about its surface. Today, we know a lot more. In more modern times, scientists have carefully mapped the Moon and sent **probes** to visit it. Astronauts have even landed there.

WHO'S WHO?

In ancient times, the people of many different cultures had gods and goddesses associated with the Moon.

GOD OR GODDESS	PLACE WORSHIPPED
Khons	Ancient Egypt
Artemis	Ancient Greece
Diana	Ancient Rome
Selena or Luna	Ancient Greece
Chandra	India
Heng-O	China
Ix Chel	Central America
Mawu	Africa
Cyolxauhqui	Mexico

THE MOON IN THE CALENDAR

As time passes, the Moon appears to change shape, from a complete disc (a Full Moon) to a thin slice, and back again. Thousands of years ago, the time between one Full Moon and the next was a measure of time. This period is equal to 29.5 days. Ancient Egyptian calendars were based on this time period, which we now call a month. There are roughly 12 New Moons a year, which is why a year has 12 months.

AMAZING FACTS

The traditional stories of many countries include tales about scary things that happen when there is a Full Moon. One example is the changing of a person into a snarling, terrifying wolf, known as a werewolf. This is said to happen in the light of a Full Moon.

In some tales, a person is supposed to turn into a savage half-human, half-wolf known as a werewolf when struck by the light of a Full Moon.

OBSERVING THE MOON

In ancient times, **astronomers** observed and recorded the movement and shape of the Moon. They tried to figure out why the Moon appears to move across the sky, how far away it is, and how big it is. Ancient Greek astronomer Hipparchus (about 190–120 BCE) was one of the first to think that the Moon was a **sphere**, rather than a flat disc.

DON'T FORGET

A Moon map is essential for any trip to the Moon. You will need one to find your landing site and to find your way from crater to crater. Maps are normally divided into the near side (which faces Earth) and the far side (which we never see).

In the book *From the Earth to the Moon*, the author Jules Verne imagined travelers being fired to the Moon inside a giant bullet.

SEEING THE SURFACE

The telescope was invented in the early 1600s. Now astronomers could see the Moon's craters for the first time. As the quality of telescopes improved, they could see more detail and began to make lunar maps. In the 1800s, the craters were named, mainly in honor of famous astronomers and scientists.

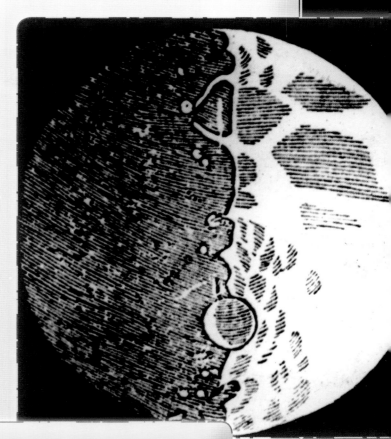

This is one of the detailed sketches of the Moon's surface made by Galileo Galilei, who in the 1600s observed the Moon though a simple telescope.

WHO'S WHO?

Galileo Galilei (1564–1642) was an Italian astronomer, mathematician, and philosopher. In 1609, Galileo heard about a new instrument called a telescope. He figured out how to make his own and quickly improved the design. He aimed his telescope at the Moon and saw that it is rough and cratered.

LUNAR PROBES

During the 1950s, the United States and the Soviet Union
(a group of countries including Russia) began launching
robot space probes to the Moon. In 1959, the Soviet
Luna 2 became the first spacecraft to reach the Moon,
where it crashed. *Luna 9* was the first spacecraft to land
in one piece. It sent the first close-up photographs of the
Moon's surface. In the 1960s, the U.S. *Surveyor* spacecraft
snapped photos of most of the Moon's surface. Later
probes brought back rock samples from the Moon.

THE FAR SIDE

The same side of the Moon (called the near side) always
faces Earth. From Earth, we cannot see the far side.
The first-ever pictures of the far side were sent back to
Earth by the Soviet probe *Luna 3*, which flew around the
Moon in 1959.

viet probe
od 1, which
on the Moon
was the first
-controlled
land on
world.

THE LATEST PROBES

Probes from the United States, China, India, and Europe continue to send us information about the Moon. The latest probes include *LRO*, a probe that is mapping the possible landing sites for manned missions, and *GRAIL*, which is helping scientists figure out what is inside the Moon.

AMAZING FACTS

In 2009, **NASA** deliberately crashed a 2-ton lump of old rocket into the Moon. Following closely behind was a probe called *LCROSS*, which flew through the cloud of **debris** thrown up. Among other things, it found water, which confirmed that there is some ice on the Moon.

This is what it would h
looked like as the *LCF*
probe approached the

MOON SCIENCE

Thanks to telescopes, space probes, and missions with crew members, we have more scientific knowledge about the Moon than about any other body in the **solar system** (except Earth, of course). This knowledge will help you during your Moon mission.

THE MOON, EARTH, AND GRAVITY

The Moon is Earth's **satellite**, and it travels around it in a path called an **orbit**. Its orbit is not a perfect circle, so the Moon moves farther away from, and closer to, Earth as it orbits. **Gravity** pulls Earth and the Moon together, and this pull keeps the Moon in orbit around Earth.

The Moon's weak gravity means that when you are on the Moon, you will be able to jump much higher than you can on Earth.

Because the Moon is so much smaller than Earth, its gravity is about one-sixth as strong as Earth's. That means an object on the Moon is pulled downward with only one-sixth of the force as it is on Earth.

MAKING THE MOON

There have been many ideas about where the Moon came from. One idea is that it was captured by Earth's gravity as it drifted by. Today, most astronomers think it was created in a giant space crash. An object about the size of Mars smashed into the young Earth, and rocky material sprayed out into space. This material slowly joined up to form the Moon.

NUMBER CRUNCHING

DIAMETER:
2,160 miles
(3,476 kilometers)

MASS (COMPARED TO EARTH):
1.23 percent of Earth's **mass**

AVERAGE DISTANCE FROM EARTH:
238,855 miles
(384,400 kilometers)

AVERAGE SURFACE TEMPERATURE:
−4°Fahrenheit (−20°Celsius)

GRAVITY:
0.17 times Earth gravity

The Moon is much smaller than Earth. The **diameter** of the Moon is just over a quarter of the diameter of Earth.

THE MOON'S PHASES

The Moon seems to change shape from day to day. Sometimes it is a complete disc, sometimes it is half a disc, and sometimes it is a thin **crescent**. Why does this happen? The Moon shines because the Sun lights up one side of it. As the Moon orbits Earth, we see different amounts of this lit side. When the Moon is on the same side of Earth as the Sun, we see little or none of the lit side. This is called a New Moon. As the Moon continues in its orbit, more and more of the lit side becomes visible. When the Moon is on the opposite side of Earth from the Sun, we see all of the lit side. This is a Full Moon.

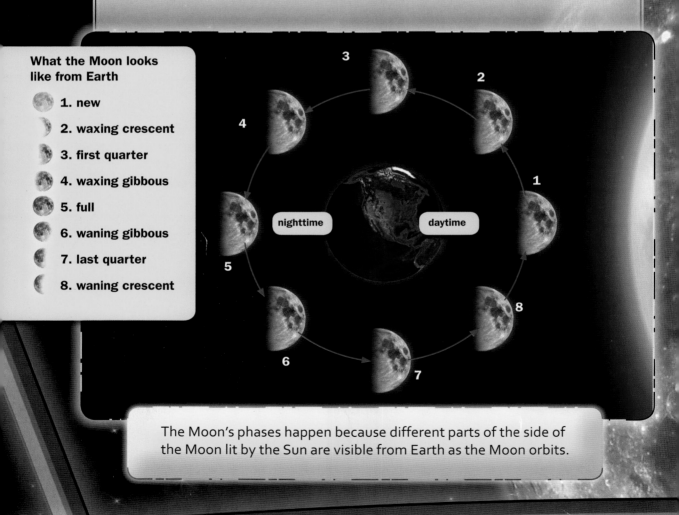

What the Moon looks like from Earth

1. new
2. waxing crescent
3. first quarter
4. waxing gibbous
5. full
6. waning gibbous
7. last quarter
8. waning crescent

nighttime   daytime

The Moon's phases happen because different parts of the side of the Moon lit by the Sun are visible from Earth as the Moon orbits.

ECLIPSES

Eclipses happen when Earth, the Moon, and the Sun line up perfectly. A solar eclipse is when the Moon comes between the Sun and Earth, and the Moon's shadow falls on Earth. A lunar eclipse is when Earth's shadow falls on the Moon.

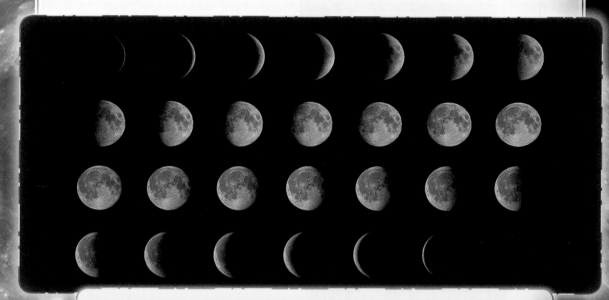

These photographs show how the Moon changes from New Moon to Full Moon and back again over one orbit around Earth.

NUMBER CRUNCHING

The Moon spins on its **axis** just once on every orbit of Earth (which takes 27.3 days). A place on the Moon gets about two weeks of daylight, then two weeks of darkness. In the day, surface temperatures rise to a roasting 260 degrees Fahrenheit (127 degrees Celsius), and in the night they fall to −279 degrees Fahrenheit (−173 degrees Celsius).

MOON ROCK

The Moon's surface is made entirely of rock and dust. The surface rock has been smashed into pieces over billions of years by numerous **meteorites**. Heating and cooling during the day and night also makes the rock break up. On Earth, in a process called the rock cycle, new rocks are always being made and old rocks are worn away. This does not happen on the Moon, so the surface does not change.

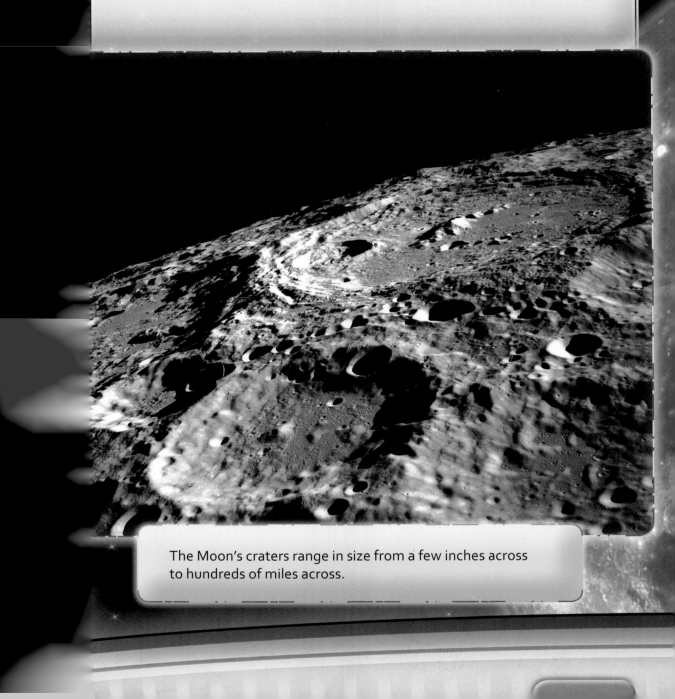

The Moon's craters range in size from a few inches across to hundreds of miles across.

SURFACE FEATURES

The Moon's craters were formed by meteorite impacts. The largest craters are called basins. Around the rim of the basins are mountains thousands of feet high. These mountains were formed from the material blasted sideways by the impacts. **Rilles** are deep canyons probably made by flowing lava. The huge dark areas on the Moon are known as *maria* (which means "seas" in Latin), although they contain no water. They were formed when giant craters were flooded by molten (liquid) rock leaking from under the Moon's crusty outer layer.

There is no **atmosphere** on the Moon. This means that there is no wind or rain to move the dust on the surface around, and so tiny craters last forever.

Footprints left in the dust on the Moon are still there, because there is no wind to disturb the dust.

INTERVIEW WITH AN ASTRONAUT

Paolo Nespoli is an Italian astronaut with the **European Space Agency (ESA)**. In 2007, Paolo went into space for 15 days, and in 2010 he spent 6 more months in space. In total, he has orbited Earth an amazing 2,782 times.

Q *Have you always wanted to be an astronaut, since you were a child?*

A Well, this was my childhood dream. When I watched the Apollo astronauts jumping on the Moon and just kind of, you know, bouncing around on the Moon, I thought, when I was a kid, "Oh, I'd like to be an astronaut!" I was lucky enough to be fascinated as a child by something that later on it turned out that I could accomplish. So, I eventually became an engineer—not because I wanted to be an astronaut or something, it's just because that was what I liked to do. I became an aerospace engineer and every time there was a space selection for an astronaut I would apply and do my best. Eventually I was lucky enough to be selected.

Q *When you're in space, especially on a long trip like you've just come back from, what food do you miss most?*

A In space there is a good amount and quantity of food, but it is very flavored. This is because in space you tend to lose a little bit of taste, and so they flavor things. There were astronauts that didn't eat because everything tasted like cardboard at the end of the mission, so they are now spicing up the food.

For me, to be honest, I found that after a couple of months, I was missing what I would call in Italy, simply, basic food. You know—spaghetti with tomato sauce. I was terribly missing a pizza. I think I was missing pizza, because I do associate pizza with, you know, going out with friends and being outside and doing things that obviously you cannot do on the space station.

Q *What other daily activities are different when you're traveling in space?*

A We don't really take a shower. We can't take a shower in space because the water goes all over the place, and, by the way, water is a very precious commodity in space and so, for example—people get a little bit astonished—we do actually recycle urine and sweat and we use it again. In space we do keep a good control on the quality of the water, and I'm pretty sure that the water that I drank in space is much safer, much cleaner, much better than what I drink at home, opening up the tap and just drinking from there.

Between 1969 and 1972, 12 astronauts in the Apollo space program landed on the Moon. The program started after U.S. President John F. Kennedy decided that the United States should try to land humans on the Moon. Years of building and testing the Apollo spacecraft and the giant *Saturn V* rocket followed.

AMAZING FACTS

The Apollo spacecraft was designed in the 1960s, only 20 years after computers had first been invented. It had computers to help the astronauts to fly it, but they were less powerful than a modern-day scientific calculator.

A *Saturn V* rocket was a towering 361 feet (110 meters) tall. The Apollo spacecraft fit into the top part of the rocket.

APOLLO AND SATURN

The Apollo spacecraft was made up of three parts. The first part was the command module, where the astronauts traveled. The service module contained a rocket motor and other equipment. The third part, the lunar module, actually landed on the Moon. NASA had to build a new rocket, called the *Saturn V,* to launch this heavy spacecraft into space.

Apollo spacecraft made several test missions before the first landing. In late 1968, *Apollo 8* carried astronauts on the first manned trip around the Moon. *Apollo 9* tested the lunar module in Earth orbit, and *Apollo 10* astronauts practiced a trip to the Moon, but did not land.

NUMBER CRUNCHING

The mission of *Apollo 8*, in 1968, lasted 147 hours and 42 seconds. The spacecraft reached a speed of 24,200 miles (38,938 kilometers) per hour —the fastest that humans had ever traveled.

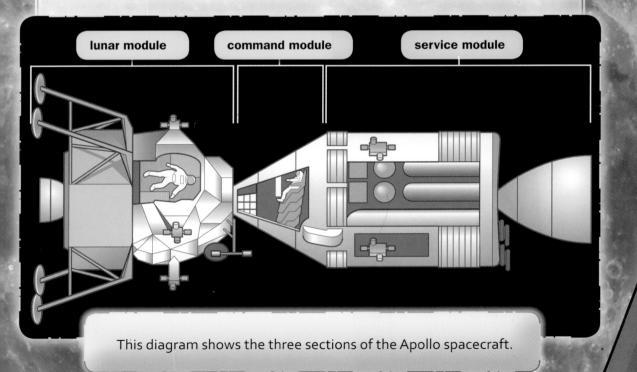

lunar module   command module   service module

This diagram shows the three sections of the Apollo spacecraft.

FIRST PEOPLE ON THE MOON

On July 16, 1969, *Apollo 11* took off from the Kennedy Space Center in Florida. On board was a crew of three astronauts: Neil Armstrong (the commander), Buzz Aldrin, and Michael Collins. Just over three days later, *Apollo 11* settled into orbit around the Moon. The next day, Armstrong and Aldrin climbed into the lunar module and descended to the surface, leaving Collins in charge of the command module.

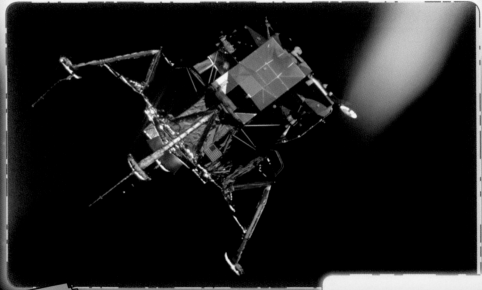

Michael Collins took this photograph of *Apollo 11*'s lunar module with Neil Armstrong and Buzz Aldrin aboard, just after they undocked from the command module.

's WHO?

n "Buzz" Aldrin (born 1930) was
nter pilot in the U.S. Air Force. He
ed training as an astronaut in 1963
made his first space flight in 1966
rd *Gemini 12*. Three years later, he
chosen as a member of the crew of
lo 11, and he became the second
on to stand on the Moon.

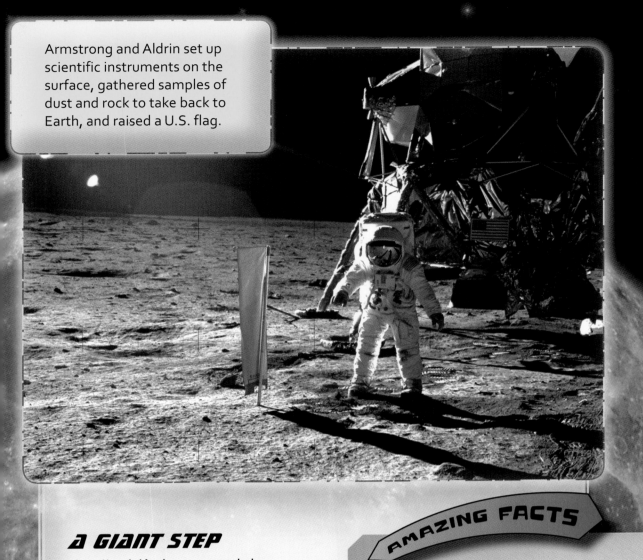

Armstrong and Aldrin set up scientific instruments on the surface, gathered samples of dust and rock to take back to Earth, and raised a U.S. flag.

A GIANT STEP

Apollo 11's lunar module, named *Eagle*, landed in the Sea of Tranquillity (one of the Moon's *maria*). A few hours later, Armstrong climbed down the ladder and jumped onto the Moon's surface. Aldrin soon followed. After just 21 hours on the Moon, Armstrong and Aldrin rejoined Collins in orbit.

AMAZING FACTS

The flight computer on *Apollo 11*'s lunar module tried to land Armstrong and Aldrin in a field of giant boulders. Armstrong quickly took control. Using precious fuel, he flew over the boulders, then a crater, before touching down. There was just 30 seconds worth of fuel left.

RETURN TO THE MOON

Six more Apollo missions followed on the success of *Apollo 11*. Each mission (except *Apollo 13*—see the box) visited a different area of the Moon. Each time, the astronauts stayed a little longer on the surface. The astronauts set up numerous experiments to find out more about the Moon and took thousands of photographs. In total, they brought 842 pounds (382 kilograms) of Moon rock back to Earth. They even had time for fun—*Apollo 14* astronaut Alan Shepard hit a golf ball on the Moon!

FINAL MISSION

Apollo 17 was the final Apollo mission. Astronauts Eugene Cernan and Harrison Schmitt stayed on the Moon's surface for nearly three Earth days. They left on December 14, 1972, with Cernan becoming the last person to leave the surface. Nobody has been to the Moon since.

AMAZING FACTS

As *Apollo 13* traveled toward the Moon, an **oxygen** tank in the service module exploded and damaged the spacecraft. The astronauts were left short of oxygen to breathe, and they were in serious danger. They used the oxygen in the lunar module and were lucky to get back to Earth alive.

You might want to take a hammer and a feather to the Moon. Why? To re-create a famous experiment. *Apollo 15* astronaut Dave Scott dropped a hammer and a feather from the same height above the surface. Both hit the surface at the same time, just as Galileo had predicted hundreds of years earlier, based on the laws of motion.

The astronauts of *Apollo 15*, *Apollo 16*, and *Apollo 17* explored the lunar surface in a battery-powered lunar roving vehicle.

PLANNING A MOON MISSION

A mission to the Moon needs extremely careful planning. When will you go? Who will go with you? Where will you land? What equipment will you take? Once that rocket blasts off, there is no going back! You could be away for more than a week, in a very **hostile** environment that is nothing like the cozy Earth that you will be leaving behind.

NASA's multi-purpose crew vehicle is being developed. In addition to traveling to the International Space Station, it may one day carry humans to Mars or to an asteroid.

SPACECRAFT AND ROCKET

Any spacecraft that takes you to the Moon must carry you and all your equipment, but it also must do many other jobs for you. The spacecraft will need a powerful rocket to lift it away from Earth's gravity. It must protect you from dangerous **radiation** from the Sun and from space, keep you warm, and provide air for you to breathe. It must also land safely on the Moon. On the return journey, it must protect you from the immense heat of re-entry into Earth's atmosphere.

During liftoff from the launch pad, the rocket will increase speed so fast that you will be pressed down into your seat. You will feel as if your body is four or five times as heavy as normal! This uncomfortable feeling only lasts a few minutes, until the spacecraft is in Earth's orbit. When the rocket motors turn off, you'll feel completely weightless.

Modern rockets, such as the *Ariane 5*, are often used to take satellites into orbit around Earth.

WHO'S GOING WITH YOU?

Who would your ideal traveling companions be? Here are some useful people you might want to come along for the ride.

CREW MEMBER:

NEIL ARMSTRONG (BORN 1930)

Neil Armstrong was a U.S. fighter pilot and **test pilot** before joining NASA to train as an astronaut in 1962. In 1969, he was chosen as commander of the *Apollo 11* mission and became the first person to stand on the Moon.

POTENTIAL JOB:

Mission commander

CREW MEMBER:

ISAAC NEWTON (1642–1727)

Isaac Newton was an English professor of mathematics. He was the first scientist to realize that things fall to the ground because of gravity. In 1687, he published *Mathematical Principles of Natural Philosophy*, which describes how gravity controls the movement of all objects in space.

POTENTIAL JOB:

Mission scientist

CREW MEMBER:

JULES VERNE (1828–1905)

In his thirties, French science-fiction writer Jules Verne quit his job to become a full-time writer. Over the next 40 years, he wrote dozens of science-fiction stories. One his most famous stories is *From the Earth to the Moon*, written in 1865.

POTENTIAL JOB:

Writing the mission diary

CREW MEMBER:

SALLY RIDE (BORN 1951)

U.S. scientist Sally Ride was chosen by NASA to train as an astronaut in 1978. On June 18, 1983, she went into space on board the space shuttle *Challenger*. She has written several children's books about being an astronaut.

POTENTIAL JOB:

Astronaut

CREW MEMBER:

JEAN-MICHEL COUSTEAU (BORN 1938)

Jean-Michel Cousteau is the son of Jacques Cousteau, the famous inventor of SCUBA diving equipment. He has explored and made movies about the ocean. He is also an environmentalist, trying to protect the oceans.

POTENTIAL JOB:

Expert on breathing equipment

WHAT TO TAKE

On a mission to the Moon, you can take some personal equipment, but there will be a strict weight limit—it was just 5 pounds (2 kilograms) each on the Apollo missions. So you might have to make some difficult choices. You might want to take a media player (with music, photos from home, and books). But forget your cell phone—there will not be a signal in space!

SUITED UP

You will need to put on a spacesuit whenever you leave your spacecraft to explore the surface of the Moon. This is probably the most complicated and expensive suit you will ever wear! Its many layers protect you from the Sun's heat and from high-speed micrometeorites. It will provide you with oxygen to breathe and keep you warm.

Astronauts performing "spacewalks" outside the International Space Station wear the sort of spacesuits that you would wear on the surface of the Moon.

FOOD AND DRINK

Some food and drink will be **dehydrated**—you can just add water and heat them up. Other food will be in cans or pouches. Only a small tank of water is carried on a spacecraft. Water is a **by-product** of the spacecraft's **fuel cells** (which are like batteries). Water is also recycled—water vapor from your breath is removed from the air and is also extracted (taken) from urine. But don't worry—it is probably cleaner than tap water on Earth!

DON'T FORGET

What memento or lucky charm would you carry with you on a Moon mission? Neil Armstrong (commander of *Apollo 11*) carried a piece of wood from a propeller of the Wright Brothers' 1903 airplane.

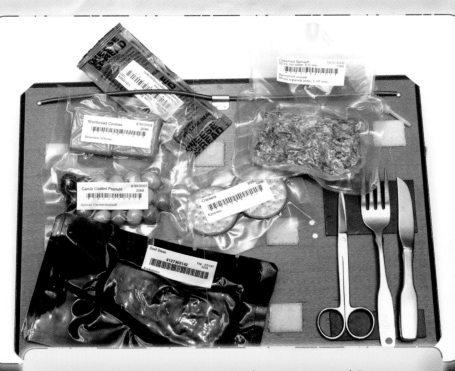

This is food for astronauts on the International Space Station, including creamed spinach and sugar-coated peanuts. It is dehydrated, to save weight and space.

SIGHTS TO SEE ON THE MOON

There are plenty of amazing sights to see on the Moon. You might be able to see some of these as your spacecraft orbits the Moon.

Tycho crater

Tycho is a ray crater. This means the rock that was thrown up by the impact is visible in lines, or "rays," of light-colored rock leading away from the crater. Tycho's rays are visible from Earth during a Full Moon.

Hadley Rille

Apollo 11 landing site

Mare Imbrium

Apennine Mountains

Tycho crater

This photograph of the near side of the Moon shows some of the best places to visit on the Moon's surface.

Mare Imbrium

The Mare Imbrium is the largest of the Moon's seas, measuring an enormous 750 miles (1,200 kilometers) across. The Mare Imbrium is surrounded by mountain chains. Mare Imbrium means "Sea of Rains," but it is actually completely dry.

Apennine Mountains

The Apennine mountain range is 373 miles (600 kilometers) long and up to 3 miles (5 kilometers) high on the edge of the Mare Imbrium (see above). It was thrown up when the Mare Imbrium was formed by a giant impact.

Hadley Rille

The Hadley Rille is a valley 84 miles (135 kilometers) long, 0.6 to 1.2 miles (1 to 2 kilometers) wide, and 1,214 feet (370 meters) deep.

Apollo 11 landing site

Visit this historic site on the edge of the Sea of Tranquillity to see the footprints of Neil Armstrong and Buzz Aldrin, the lower section of *Eagle*, their lunar lander, and all the equipment they left behind.

DON'T FORGET

As your spacecraft orbits the Moon before landing, watch out for Earth coming up over the Moon's **horizon**—just as you can see the Moon rise from Earth.

INTERVIEW WITH A SPACE SCIENTIST

John Spencer is a NASA scientist. He works mainly on the Cassini mission, which is exploring the moons of Saturn, as well as Saturn itself. His team plans where *Cassini* spacecraft will go and what information it will gather.

Q **Do you think we will ever have human colonies in space?**

A I think it's possible, but it's only possible if we can make space travel a lot cheaper than it is now. To get a colony where six people can live on the International Space Station—we can barely afford that. It's going to be a long way in the future, I think. It's certainly not the way I thought it would be when I was 12 years old watching the Apollo astronauts on the Moon and imagining that by now we would have huge space colonies and people would be exploring the moons of Jupiter.

Q *Do you have any space heroes?*

A People like Eugene Shoemaker who was a geologist, and who was one of the first people to get interested in impact craters and to understand how you can learn about craters on the Moon by studying craters on Earth. He was one of the first people to really figure out the geology of the Moon. It was amazing what he did and I was privileged enough to get to know him.

My original inspiration was those Apollo astronauts going off and walking on the surface of the Moon. It blew my mind when I was a kid that it was possible for people to do that, just to imagine them being so far away. I was just old enough to really get it, how amazing it was.

Q *Why do you think it is important that we study space?*

A Well, you know, you can spend your life in your house, or you can get out and get to know your neighborhood. And that's what we're doing. We're just learning amazing things about our own planet as we do so. For example, we see all these craters on the Moon, and once we realized that those weren't volcanoes, those were produced by things smashing into the Moon, then you realize that, well, that must have happened to Earth as well. So, that really changes how you think about the history of Earth. Earth was pummeled early in its history and would have been covered in craters in the way the Moon is, and no one would have thought of that if we hadn't gone and explored and figured out what all these holes in the ground on the Moon were.

ON THE MOON

The Moon's surface is a hostile environment. Remember that there is no atmosphere, and it can be roasting hot or freezing cold. You will spend most of your time inside your spacecraft, perhaps doing some science experiments and eating and sleeping. When you go outside to walk across the dusty surface—this is called an extra-vehicular activity (EVA)—you will have to put on your spacesuit.

A SHORT STAY

All the basic things you take for granted at home will be missing on the Moon. That includes air to breathe, water to drink, and food to eat. Electricity will come from **solar panels** and fuel cells, so the supply is limited. This means that you cannot stay on the Moon for more than a few days before returning—otherwise supplies will begin to run out.

DON'T FORGET

Harmful rays from the Sun and from space hit the Moon all the time. You will have to wear a device called a dosimeter, which measures how much radiation has hit you during your time outside. If your dose gets too high, you will have to stay inside your spaceship.

WHEN TO VISIT

Whatever your destination on the Moon, don't forget that there will be about two weeks of daylight, followed by two weeks of darkness. So choose your landing spot in a place where it will be daytime. Otherwise you will see nothing, your solar panels will not work, and it will be extremely cold. Any time of year will be fine, because there are no seasons on the Moon.

You will want to take plenty of snapshots of the Moon. Here, astronaut Richard Gordon takes photos of the Moon from the command module of *Apollo* 12, in 1969.

LIVING ON THE MOON

Living on the Moon for more than a few days would be very difficult. You would need a permanent base rather than a spacecraft. This could be made from parts sent from Earth by remote-controlled spacecraft. Like a spacecraft, the base would protect you from the dangers of space.

This is one of NASA's ideas for a permanent Moon base. It would be near one of the Moon's poles, where nights are short.

For a long stay on the Moon, you would need to make use of Moon materials. Ice has been found near the Moon's poles, and this could be collected for water. Water is made up of hydrogen and oxygen, so the oxygen could be taken out and used to breathe. A base would probably be set up at one of the Moon's poles, where there is permanent sunlight to run solar panels for electricity. Food could be supplied from Earth at first, but then it would need to be grown in special greenhouses.

RETURN TO THE MOON

Several countries around the world have plans to send astronauts to the Moon in the future, but there are no definite dates yet. Getting to the Moon is a very complex and hugely expensive task, and it will probably be 2025 at the earliest before astronauts land there again. It will be many more years before any sort of Moon base is established.

AMAZING FACTS

The European Space Agency (ESA) is taking a new approach to Moon exploration. It is experimenting with a robot astronaut named Justin, which is being tested on the International Space Station. Justin could eventually visit the Moon instead of human astronauts.

MAP OF THE SOLAR SYSTEM

MERCURY

VENUS

EARTH

MARS

ASTEROID BELT

JUPITER

SATURN

URANUS

NEPTUNE

The sizes of the planets and their distances from the Sun are not to scale. To show all the planets' real distances from the Sun, this page would have to be over half a mile long!

TIMELINE

100s BCE
The ancient Greek astronomer Hipparchusis is one of the first people to decide that the Moon is a sphere.

1600s
The invention of the telescope allows astronomers such as Galileo Galilei to see the Moon's surface in detail for the first time.

1959
The space probe *Luna 2* is the first spacecraft to reach the Moon, where it crashes.
Luna 3 sends pictures of the far side of the Moon back to Earth.

1962
President John F. Kennedy announces that the United States plans to send astronauts to the Moon by 1970.

1966
Luna 9 is the first probe to land on the Moon.

1968
Apollo 8 carries astronauts around the Moon for the first time.

1969
Apollo 11 lands on the Moon with astronauts Neil Armstrong and Buzz Aldrin.

1970
Apollo 13 returns safely to Earth after an explosion on board on the way to the Moon.

1972
Astronauts from *Apollo 17* visit the Moon. No astronauts have been to the Moon since.

2009
The probe *LCROSS* flies into a cloud of dust thrown up by deliberately crashing an old rocket into the Moon's surface.

FACT FILE

DIAMETER:
2,160 miles
(3,476 kilometers)

AVERAGE DISTANCE FROM EARTH:
238,855 miles
(384,400 kilometers)

SMALLEST DISTANCE FROM EARTH:
221,463 miles
(356,410 kilometers)

FURTHEST DISTANCE FROM EARTH:
252,710 miles
(406,697 kilometers)

TIME FOR ONE ORBIT OF EARTH:
27 Earth days, 7 hours,
43 minutes

DAY LENGTH:
29 Earth days, 12 hours,
44 minutes

AVERAGE SURFACE TEMPERATURE:
–4 °F (–20 °C)

HIGHEST SURFACE TEMPERATURE:
260 °F (127 °C)

LOWEST SURFACE TEMPERATURE:
–279 °F (–173 °C)

GRAVITY:
0.17 times Earth gravity

LARGEST CRATER:
South Pole–Aitken Basin,
diameter 1,616 miles
(2,600 kilometers)

FIRST SPACE PROBE TO CRASH ONTO THE MOON:
Luna 2 (1959)

FIRST SPACECRAFT TO LAND ON THE MOON:
Luna 9 (1966)

FIRST LUNAR ROVER:
Lunokhod 1 (1970)

FIRST ASTRONAUTS ON THE MOON:
Neil Armstrong and Buzz
Aldrin, *Apollo 11* (1969)

GLOSSARY

astronomer person who studies space

atmosphere layer of gases surrounding a planet

axis line through a planet or moon that the planet or moon spins around. It always goes through the planet or moon's poles.

by-product useful product that is made during the manufacture of another product

canyon valley with very steep or vertical sides

crater dish-shaped hole in the surface of a planet, made by a meteorite smashing into the surface

crescent curved shape with two pointed ends

debris loose material, such as small pieces of broken rock

dehydrated dried out

diameter distance from one side of a circle or sphere to the other

European Space Agency (ESA) European organization involved in space research and exploration

fuel cell device that makes electricity by mixing two chemicals (such as oxygen and hydrogen)

gravity force that pulls objects toward each other. Big objects, such as planets, have much stronger gravity than smaller objects, such as people.

horizon line between the ground (or sea) and the sky

hostile unfriendly and dangerous

lava molten rock that flows on the surface of a planet

lunar relating to the Moon

maria huge, dark areas on the Moon (the word means "seas" in Latin)

mass measure of the amount of material that makes up an object

meteorite piece of rock from space that hits the surface of a planet or moon

NASA short for "National Aeronautics and Space Administration," the U.S. space agency

orbit path of a planet or other satellite around a larger body, such as the Sun

oxygen gas that we need to breathe to stay alive, and one of the gases in Earth's atmosphere

probe robot spacecraft sent to visit planets, moons, and other objects in the solar system

radiation particles and rays that come from some objects in space, such as stars. Some types of radiation are harmful to humans.

rille narrow channel or canyon in the surface of a planet or Moon

satellite object, often human-made, that orbits a larger object

solar panel device that makes electricity from sunlight

solar system the Sun, the planets that orbit around the Sun, their moons, and other objects that orbit the Sun, such as asteroids and comets

sphere perfectly round, ball-shaped object

telescope device that makes distant objects look bigger

test pilot pilot who flies new types of aircraft to make sure they work properly

FIND OUT MORE

BOOKS

Bond, Peter. *DK Guide to Space* (DK Guides). New York: Dorling Kindersley, 2006.

Goldsmith, Mike. *Solar System* (Discover Science). New York: Macmillan, 2010.

Grego, Peter. *Exploring the Moon* (QEB Space Guides). North Mankato, Minn: QEB, 2007.

Landau, Elaine. *The Moon* (True Books). New York: Children's Press, 2008.

Oxlade, Chris. *The Earth and Its Moon* (Earth and Space). New York: Rosen Central, 2008.

Ross, Stewart. *Moon*. New York: Scholastic, 2009.

DVDS

Apollo 13 (Universal Pictures, 1995; 2005)
The Universe (A&E, 2010)

INTERNET SITES

FactHound offers a safe, fun way to find internet sites related to this book. All of the sites on FactHound have been researched by our staff.

Here's all you do:

Visit *www.facthound.com*

Type in this code: 9781410945723

PLACES TO VISIT

Hayden Planetarium
Central Park West and 79th Street, New York, N.Y. 10024
www.haydenplanetarium.org

Kennedy Space Center
SR 405, Kennedy Space Center, Florida 32899
www.nasa.gov/centers/kennedy

Smithsonian National Air and Space Museum
Independence Ave. at 7th St. SW, Washington, D.C. 20560
www.nasm.si.edu

FURTHER RESEARCH

Here are some starting points for finding out more about the Moon:

- Look at the Moon in the night sky, with the naked eye and through binoculars. Try to identify some of the seas and craters with the help of a Moon map.
- Research some of the ideas about how the Moon was made.
- Look at images and videos of solar and lunar eclipses.
- Follow the progress of the latest missions of probes to the Moon.
- Find out about living in zero gravity.
- Find out more about the story of *Apollo 13*.

INDEX

Aldrin, Buzz 22, 23, 33
ancient peoples 6–7, 8
Apollo missions 20–25, 30, 33, 35, 37, 42
Ariane 5 rocket 27
Armstrong, Neil 22, 23, 28, 31, 33
astronauts 6, 12, 18–25, 28, 29, 39
astronomers 8, 9, 42
atmosphere 17, 27
axis 15

basins 17

calendars 7
canyons 5, 17
Cassini missions 34
Cernan, Eugene 24
Collins, Michael 22
colonies in space 34
command module 21, 22
Cousteau, Jean-Michel 29
craters 4, 5, 9, 16, 17, 32, 35, 43
crescent Moon 14

days and nights 14, 15, 37, 38, 43

Earth 12, 13, 14, 15, 16, 33, 35, 40
eclipses 15
European Space Agency (ESA) 18, 39
extra-vehicular activity (EVA) 36

far side of the Moon 10
first Moon landing 22–23
food 19, 31, 39
footprints 17, 33
formation of the Moon 13
fuel cells 31, 36
Full Moon 7, 14, 15

Galileo Galilei 9, 25
GRAIL space probe 11
gravity 12–13, 28, 43

Hipparchus 8

ice 11, 39
International Space Station 30, 34, 39

Kennedy, John F. 20

lava 5
LCROSS space probe 11
LRO space probe 11
Luna space probes 10
lunar eclipse 15
lunar maps 8, 9
lunar module 21, 22, 23, 24, 33
lunar roving vehicles (LRVs) 10, 25
Lunokhod 2 rover 10

Mare Imbrium 33
meteorites 16, 17, 30
Moon base 38–39
mountains 5, 17, 33
multi-purpose crew vehicle 26

NASA 11, 21, 26, 34, 38
Nespoli, Paolo 18–19
New Moon 14, 15
Newton, Isaac 28

orbit 12, 14, 15, 27, 43
Outer Space Treaty 5
oxygen 24, 39

phases 14

radiation 27, 36
Ride, Sally 29
rills 17, 33
robots 39
rock 16, 24, 32
rock cycle 16

satellites 12, 27
Saturn V rocket 20, 21
science fiction 8, 29
Sea of Tranquillity 23, 33
seas 4, 5, 17, 33
service module 21, 24
Shepard, Alan 24
Shoemaker, Eugene 35
solar eclipse 15
solar panels 36, 37, 39
solar system 40–41
South Pole-Aitken basin 17
space probes 6, 10–11, 42
space scientists 34–35
space shuttles 29
spacesuits 30
spacewalks 30
Spencer, John 34–35
Sun 14, 15, 36
Surveyor space probe 10

telescopes 6, 9
temperatures 13, 15, 43
Tycho 32

Verne, Jules 8, 29

water 11, 19, 31, 39
weightlessness 27
werewolves 7
Wright Brothers 31

years 7